Pocket CARDI B Wisdom

INSPIRATIONAL QUOTES AND WISE
WORDS FROM THE QUEEN OF RAP

Hardie Grant

BOOKS

CONTENTS

CARDI B
on being

gular

Degular Shmegular

"I'm so free-spirited ...
everyone has a me
inside them, that loud
girl that just wanna
go 'ayyyy!'...

**... No matter if you
a doctor, a lawyer,
a teacher, it comes out.
Like, aha, I got you being
yourself for a lil two
minutes or three, huh?"**

"That soap gave me the yeast infection of 2017!"

"You know all these female rappers, they talking about they money, they talking about they cars, so it's like, what's something that I enjoy? I enjoy fights!"

"All right, here's the thing, when I was 21, I did not have enough meat on my body ...

... If I was to get lipo, I wouldn't have fat for my ass."

**On main character Winter Santiaga,
from *The Coldest Winter Ever*
by Sister Souljah:**

"It's a hood book,
but it's really good ...

... The main character is like my alter ego. She is a bad girl. I like a bit of bad-girl shit."

"I'm the person who has to prove everyone wrong, constantly. Constantly."

"I love government.
I'm obsessed
with presidents. I'm
obsessed to know how
the system works."

"I work with
somebody who gives
me compliments all day,
and I'm like ...

... Oh, my gosh, can you just stop?"

"I'm too nervous,
I'm too shy. When I met
Beyoncé, people be like,
'How that felt? ...

... I bet you
was mad happy'
... it's like, 'Actually,
I wanted to shit
on myself.'"

"Nobody makes my decisions about my life but me."

"Just because I'm out there and very sexual doesn't mean that I have to be whorish."

"When I talk, I make a lot of mistakes. Like, I might say words, and the words are not even in the dictionary ...

... But people still like it because you can tell that I'm saying it from the heart."

"People be asking me:
'Are you a model, are you
a comedian?' Nah, I ain't
none of that. I'm a ho!"

"Having a number one song makes me happy — but working for it makes me really happy."

"I used to tell myself that I will always be myself ...

... Little by little, I'm feeling like I'm getting trapped and muted."

CARDI B on

Bronx

Pride

"There's no hood hooder than my hood."

"I love my career now, but it's like my spirit was happier before. When I was dancing, I had so much fun. I felt powerful in the club. I felt free."

"**Everybody got different beliefs and different religions and were raised differently, yet you also supposed to be careful you don't offend somebody ...**

... Everybody gets bothered about everything. Everybody got a fucking opinion about you. You always got to filter yourself."

On her distinct accent:

"That's my biggest problem, that takes me a long time in the booth. I be trying to pronounce words properly and without an accent ...

... Each and every song from my album, I most likely did it over five times, because I'm really insecure about my accent when it comes to music. In person, I don't care."

"My features ... my nose,
my lips, the little bit
of colour that I have,
my hair texture ...

... it didn't come
from two white people
f**king each other."

On her career as a stripper:

"A lot of women here, they taught me to be more powerful, I did gain, like, a passion and love [for] performing ...

... It made me feel pretty ... I'm glad for this chapter in my life."

"One thing I could say:
Being in a gang don't make
you not one dollar ...

... And I know for a fact every gang member, he asking himself, 'Why did I turn this?'"

CARDI B on

and *Offset*

On plastic surgery, post-baby:

"I'm not even going to call it surgery, I'm just going to say a 'titty renovation.'"

On being on tour
during her birthday:

"I was sad, because
it's like, 'Oh, my gosh,
I'm not getting no d**k
on my birthday.'"

"I need to make money for my family and my future family. I'm not a YOLO person ...

... I think 25 years from now. I think about my future kids, future husband, future house."

"**While I was pregnant, I kept telling myself, I can't wait till I'm back out there. I'm going to look hot, and I'm going to be *that bitch*.**"

"I feel like moms who
do wanna feel sexy can
be. I don't feel like once
you become a mom, you
supposed to be this nun."

"People don't really
talk about what you go
through after pregnancy.
Like, they don't tell you
that you get stitches
down there ...

... Or that
your first two weeks
you're constipated. Or
that you get contractions
because of breastfeeding.
I wasn't expecting that."

"When Kulture was
born, I felt like I was
a kid again; everything
was making me cry,
and I needed a lot of
love. I be feeling like,
'Do babies know who's
they mom?' ...

... I feel like babies love whoever is giving them the milk, and I want to give the milk the whole time. I want her to *know* me."

On being a wife and mother:

"You don't lose street cred, but people want an illusion that female artists are available ...

**... They fantasise less
when they know they
actually somebody's wife.
And then imagine
having a baby."**

On her first date with Offset:

"Around Super Bowl time I told my publicist to tell him, because I was very shy, 'Listen, if we gonna go on a public date together ...

... you cannot make me
look like a dumb-ass
after this.' I never
wanted to date a rapper
because I would hate
to look crazy in public."

"Sometimes I'll see something online and it'll piss me off, and then my baby will start crying or something ...

... and it's like, 'You know what? I've got to deal with the milk. Forget this.'"

"I love her, she's like my little best friend ...

... She just makes the gloomiest days like sunshine. I love it. It's a slice of heaven."

CARDI B on

Bardi

Mania

"When I do music, I don't feel like it's competition. Then again, it kinda is, but I don't like thinking like that ...

... and I don't understand why they do that to women, and especially women in hip-hop."

"If you go broke and lose
your career, it's bad —
and everybody is talkin'
shit about it! ...

... At least if you lose your 9-to-5 you don't got millions of people judging you and talking shit while you lost your job."

"I don't want to influence women to do something — I want you to feel that empowerment, like you *could* do that."

"This generation loves to get high. They love to be on drugs. This is why they on that shit: they don't want to think about what you're saying."

"People think they smart. Some people think being a feminist is having a degree, having a very high vocabulary, and it's not ...

... It's a woman who thinks she has the same rights as men."

"People always be like, 'Oh, Cardi never used to rep it when she wasn't making music.' Yeah, because I already got signed. I can do that now. I'm smarter than what people think ...

... **There's so many things that I limited myself because I wanted a million-dollar contract. When I do interviews, I don't talk about it, because I will lose my endorsements.**"

**On Hollywood men who have
embraced the #MeToo Movement:**

"These producers and directors, they're not woke, they're scared."

"If I want to get cool points, I could take a picture with a thong and my ass and y'all gonna give me the same amount of likes. I'm gonna trend even bigger."

"I'm always watching
the news. I'm always
looking at it on my phone.
I hate when you talk about
something that's going on
in the community, people
think, because you're
famous, you doing
it for clout …

... But you concerned
about it because you
are a citizen of America;
you are a citizen
of the world."

"At first people didn't want to play my music, a lot of DJs were sleeping on me. I had to keep making music until I found the right hit ...

... I wanted them
to take me seriously,
but they were fronting
on the kid."

CARDI B on

Sh

"People want me to be
so full of shame that
I used to dance. I would
never be ashamed of it.
I made a lot of money,
I had a good time and
it showed me a lot ...

... it made me open my eyes about how people are, how men are, about hunger and passion and ambition."

"A lot of people wonder,
'Why would anybody
want to be a dancer?'...

Shmoney

... Because there's money!"

"No man wants to accept
they could be getting
used for money, but it's
OK for them to let us
know that they use us? ...

... It's in their lyrics, in the way they act."

"I feel like my life
is a fairy tale and I'm
a princess — rags to
riches, people trying
to sabotage ...

... Before, I cared about everything — relationship, gossip. Now I don't feel like I have the time to please people."

"A lot of people always want to make fun of me — 'Oh, you used to be a stripper!' — I don't ever regret it, because I learned a lot. I feel like it matured me ...

... My biggest ambition was money. That's what these women put in my head: nothing is important but the money."

On having 5 cars and no driving license:

"You know how many things I can rap about now that I own these cars? ...

... I couldn't rap about them before, but now I can."

Sources

'Cardi B Carpool Karaoke', 2018, *The Late Late Show with James Corden*, youtube.com - pp. 78-79, pp. 92-93

'Cardi B on Strict Parenting and Being a Sexy Mom', 2019, *Harper's Bazaar*, harpersbazaar.com - p. 49

Collins, H. 2018, 'why the whole world is talking about cardi b', *Vice*, i-d.vice.com - p. 30

Grigoriadis, V. 2019, 'Cardi B Opens Up About Her "Rags to Riches" Cinderella Story', *Harper's Bazaar*, harpersbazaar.com - pp. 16-17, p. 20, p. 21, pp. 58-59, pp. 88-89

Heller, C. 2019, 'Cardi B Gushes About Daughter Kulture and Parenthood: "I'm a Good Mom"', *E! News*, eonline.com - p. 60-61

Hughes, H. 2018, 'Cardi B Revisits Her Roots and Her Old Strip Club in New Interview: "I'm Glad For This Chapter in My Life"', *Billboard*, billboard.com, pp. 22-23, pp. 38-39, pp. 90-91

Hughes, J. 2018, 'Cardi B Gives Her Most Explicit Interview Yet', *Cosmopolitan*, cosmopolitan.com - p. 24, p. 25, p. 31, pp. 32-33, pp. 36-37, p. 74

Macpherson, A. 2017, '"I want you to feel that empowerment": how Cardi B went from stripper to star', *The Guardian*, theguardian.com - pp. 6-7, pp. 64-65, p. 68, pp. 70-71, p. 82-83, pp. 86-87

Solway, D. 2018, 'Cardi B Gets Candid: Hip-Hop's Fiercest Female Rapper Speaks Out About Her Past, Her Career, and Being a New Mom', *W magazine*, wmagazine.com - p. 14, p. 44, p. 48, pp. 50-51, pp. 52-53, pp. 54-55

Spanos, B. 2017, 'The Year of Cardi B', *Rolling Stone*, rollingstone.com - p. 8, p. 9, p. 45, pp. 26-27, pp. 46-47, pp. 66-67, p. 69, pp. 84-85

Weaver, C. 2018, 'Cardi B's Money Moves', *GQ magazine*, gq.com - p. 15, pp. 10-11, pp. 34-35, pp. 72-73, p. 75, pp. 76-77

Pocket Cardi B Wisdom

Published in 2019 by Hardie Grant Books,
an imprint of Hardie Grant Publishing

Hardie Grant Books (London)
5th & 6th Floors
52-54 Southwark Street
London SE1 1UN

Hardie Grant Books (Melbourne)
Building 1, 658 Church Street
Richmond, Victoria 3121

hardiegrantbooks.com

British Library Cataloguing-in-Publication Data. A catalogue
record for this book is available from the British Library.

ISBN: 978-1-78488-316-4

Publishing Director: Kate Pollard
Senior Editor: Molly Ahuja
Junior Editor: Eila Purvis
Design: Jim Green
Cover Illustrator: Michele Rosenthal
Colour Reproduction by p2d
Printed and bound in China by Leo Paper Products Ltd.